Sleeping Alone

Sleeping Alone

Michael Thorley

Indigo

Acknowledgements

I wish to thank Beverley George, editor of *Eucalypt* and, previously, *Yellow Moon*, for permission to reprint here the tanka sequence 'Five Beads', several of the tanka, and the poems 'On the Coolamon Road', 'The Jogger Justifies His Anzac Day', 'Senior Aquarobics' and 'Rainbow Lorikeets'.
Several of the tanka were subsequently published in *Ribbons – The Journal of the American Tanka Society*.

Thanks

I wish to thank Martin Dolan, Sue Edgar and Melinda Smith
for their inexhaustible and invaluable encouragement and support;
John Foulcher and Kathy Kituai for the courses
which firmed my feet on this poetic road;
Geoff Page for providing the opportunities to read
at Bees&co and The Gods;
Geoff Page and Alan Gould for reviewing this manuscript
and providing advice towards its publication;
Anne Langridge for her valuable advice on design and layout;
Beverley George for her insights, encouragement and considerable
support with the writing and publication of my tanka (and other verse);
Amelia Fielden for her informative and inspiring courses on tanka
writing; and all the kind friends who listened and appreciated.

Sleeping Alone
ISBN 978 1 74027 498 2
Copyright © text Michael Thorley 2008
Copyright © cover design Anne Langridge 2002

An Indigo book first published 2008
Reprinted 2016

Ginninderra Press
PO Box 3461 Port Adelaide 5015
www.ginninderrapress.com.au

For Pam

Contents

Sleeping Alone	9
Black Cockatoos in the Rain	10
Cleaving	11
Christmas Eve	12
Fix	13
Things	14
Wanting To Tell You	15
Lipsticks	16
Photograph	17
Grief – 1	18
Grief – 2	19
Footsteps	20
Afterwards – A Tanka Sequence	21
Anniversary	22
Dining Alone	23
Five Beads – A Tanka Sequence	24
On the Coolamon Road	25
The Ward	26
In a Motel	27
On the Lake	28
Views of the Opera House	29
Mowing	30
Baggage	31
Bowlers	32
Reflections	33
The Jogger Justifies His Anzac Day	34
Nashos	35
The Advance	36
Spit Polishing	37
Sandakan Memorial	38
Stars	39

On First Looking into Slater's Guide	40
Racing Pigeons	41
Owl	42
Rainbow Lorikeets	43
Heron	44
Sonnet For Sixty – 2005	45
Retiring	46
Tanka	48
Seasons	49
Leaves	50
The Senior Aquarobics Class	51
98	52
Two Women	53
Last Years – A Tanka Sequence	54
To a Friend	56
Tanka	57
Professional Encounter	58
Ticket Not To Ride	59
Moon	61
Trophies	63
Bait	64
If	65
Lines	66
Riddle	67
Deceased Estate	68
The Kingdom of Heaven	69
Everyday Odysseus	70
Cosmology – 1	71
Cosmology – 2	72
Aspirational	73
Pears	74
Simplify! Simplify!	75

Sleeping Alone

The bed is warm, but not with warmth of you,
though you delighted in this switched-on heat.
I only need one pillow, still keep two,
and miss the questing iciness of feet.
I rub my hands, but not to abdicate
responsibility, nor wring more grief:
the dry, cold air of winter desiccates,
and cream you made me use still brings relief.
I switch the bed lamp off, and darkness comes.
Once, you softened darkness, sharing night.
Your Panda and your Petal Bear, though dumb,
do what they can to make dark's burden light.
But when you come in dreams, I wake to pain,
half-wishing that I'd slept alone again.

Black Cockatoos in the Rain

You saw them first,
the black cockatoos,
landing in our gum
like a flock of shadows.

Feathers spiked by rain
they whistled, moaned,
complaining
at their circumstance.

They loped, floated
from branch to branch;
nipped buds, twigs, nuts,
raining them down.

One swung insolently
by its beak, another
spread wings, became
a cross, turned

cheeks painted
with yellow suns,
spread its tail and shrieked
a black prophecy.

After this they left;
we went inside.
What else to do but do
the things we always do?

Cleaving

I remember the night
exactly

I came in the door
you just off the phone

'The doctor rang,' you said,
'a problem…'

we hugged
to share the fear

and entered
separate worlds

Christmas Eve

A summer afternoon, the warm air still,
our courtyard elder casting nets of shade.
You read; I watch as insects flick through sun;
like tiny shooting stars they flare and fade.

It's Christmas Eve, and you're not very well.
Our silence shrouds the Christmases to come.
A long strand of web, drifting loose,
just for a moment brightens, in this sun.

Fix

streetwise now
she suffers the needle
hunting
her blue streams

you have beautiful veins
says the nurse
(who surreptitiously appraises
everyone's veins)

we're hoping
for a fix
suspect
there isn't one

she works hard
at being an addict
this stuff she's on
gives very few highs

perhaps one day
she'll kick the habit
withdrawal though
can be a killer

and death the dealer
leads her on
knowing he's onto
a sure thing

Things

After their owners die, things die too;
without their animating spirits seem
to fret and sag: sewing baskets, unrummaged,
gather dust; books await
the mass graves of charity bins,
or stand like soldiers on parade
for whom the orders never come; clothes
are packed away, or hang in cupboards
preserving precious scent;
letters, stranded, lie in coffin boxes,
where silverfish glide like ghosts
across the yellowing pages, nibbling gossip
and faded love. Sometimes spiders come
and wrap things up, and I don't bother them
for fear of memories fluttering out like moths.
Others find new life in cast-off stores,
or in the homes of friends.
Shell of the old, these things line my life,
holding on to me as I let go.

Wanting To Tell You

the orchids bloomed again and again last summer
and the bulbs you planted came up

wanting to tell you

I can't work out how you folded things
to keep the linen cupboard so tidy

wanting to tell you

I can't bear to give your clothes away
and keeping the wardrobes shut preserves your scent

wanting to tell you

how sad it was when things we'd had for years
broke or stopped working

wanting to tell you

there are still two toothbrushes in the cup
and your lipsticks are lined up neatly along their shelf

wanting to tell you

our garden never ran out of flowers
to put beside your grave

wanting to tell you

the problem is – and you'd smile at this –
I just keep on

wanting to tell you

Lipsticks

I keep them
your lipsticks

Shiseido, Clinique
Marie-Christine

they lie along
the bathroom shelf

tints of fuchsia
carmine, mauve

palette to colour
each day's moods

bullets to arm
each night's kiss

I treasure now
these shapes you mouthed

shading lips
to stamp your love

a twist, they curl
into their shells

the lids
click on

sweet honey, waterlily
rouge chanteur

I lay them out
my pretty coffins.

Photograph

A grey path runs beside the metal lake
past empty winter trees. You are there,
a tiny figure with your back to me,
walking away, your red jacket bright,
and the only coloured thing. This photograph
one of the last I have of you. We walked
together on that path so many times
to where it curves away, and out of sight.

Grief – 1

Cry? Of course I cry – is there a choice?
Not to cry is to insult the years.
Would you have the joy without the pain?
Love demands an equal weight in tears.

Grief – 2

I've grieved
by the book

viewed
cried
hugged
talked
prayed

OK?

So, now
can I stop?

Footsteps

in the corridor
outside the hospital chapel

clip-clop
of high heels

tread
of leather shoes

squeak
of sneakers

and a slow
slipper-shuffle

pausing
just near the door

Afterwards – A Tanka Sequence

two brushes
in the toothbrush cup
mine and yours –
how long, I wonder
till I say goodbye

that stuck door
opened for the first time
since you died –
in a sudden breeze
voice of your wind-chimes

after two years
came back to the coffee lounge
seeking us –
just like my memories
renovations here too

death's door
for most of my life
shut tight –
until you passed through
and left it ajar

remembering –
I watch fallen leaves
swirl in the wind –
just for a moment
alive one more time

Anniversary

Once more I'm drawn to the hospital's small
agnostic chapel: four years.
The room is empty, quiet now.
There was, a while ago, a doctor,
who brought his kneeling pad and said his prayers
facing Mecca, which was somewhere out
from the corner of the room;
and two people came and whispered together
in German, I think, and left. Now, silence;
until, from somewhere nearby,
the lively chatter of starlings come home for the night.
Outside in the corridor conversations pass,
and the brisk clip-clop of a woman's high heels.
Silence comes; the day moves to twilight.
I watch the long translucent window
darkening toward the hour you died;
the hour we switched off the machine,
making your death official; at last
taking away the tubes, the artificial breath,
giving you back your dignity, as if
casting you off on voyages to come.
Dusk; soon the dinner trolleys will clatter past,
the polishers whine, and the night staff
and visitors come. The chapel is still,
and seems to wait for something to happen.
The hour passes. I gather up my things
and go out into the dark, avoiding Emergency,
to where my car is parked. Straight ahead
the windows of the chemo clinic
are brightly lit, but the staff and patients gone.
I start the engine, reverse and drive away.
I've asked a friend to come around for tea.

Dining Alone

When I'm dining alone
the waiter always
removes the cutlery
that would have been yours.

'Dining alone, sir?'
(just half a question)
and I would be left,
clearly dining alone.

Perhaps I should be saying,
'No, there's someone there;
leave the things a while,
we'd like to talk.'

rather than meekly
sitting there
and letting them take you away
again and again.

(After reading a poem, 'Anniversary', by Stephen McInerney)

Five Beads – A Tanka Sequence

sometimes
remembering you
I visit church –
offer a rosary
of doubtful prayers

I choose times
when the side chapel
is empty –
listening to silence
for more than silence

I ask
like old Thomas
for a sign –
the Virgin's statue
looks down with blank eyes

can't stop
these rituals learned
long ago –
beads counting out
my best intentions

leaving
I light a candle
for you –
twenty cents buys
a little of heaven

On the Coolamon Road

A fibro farmhouse out on the Coolamon road
for seven bucks a week became my home;
a place of dismantled lives, of sheds of junk,
and a 'squat' for mice and spiders – I lived on edge
as hand-sized huntsmen skimmed around the walls,
or lurked on doors or beds to smile 'surprise!'
At night the mice came out to leap and squeal,
and share my food. (One died in my piano;
I didn't think my playing was that bad.)
But bigger beasts would roam – the fearsome cows
bellowed and crashed through the head-high thistle patch;
I listened in awe; what had become of 'moo'?
Nights brought silence, vast and still, the kind
the city never knows. Uncurtained windows
showed me empty paddocks white with moon
or smothering dark; my little lantern house
made me feel observed by unknown eyes,
and every sound I made went echoing.
One night a galvanised iron sheet crashed;
then nothing, no one. I trembled in my dreams.
Each day brought reassuring sun and noise:
the creak of the house as timbers stretched awake,
and squealing galahs scraping the iron roof.
On Saturdays I'd wash; hang out the clothes
on a rise behind the house; swept by wind
they dried in minutes; I took the armfuls in,
embracing the gathered warmth of sun and sky.
A flat came up in town; I weighed things up;
dismantled my farmhouse fears, stacked the shed,
and closed the gate upon the Coolamon Road.

The Ward

In Emergency it starts – with talk
of pacemakers, but then they baulk:
'She's much too old' (She'll soon be dead.)
'We'll make her comfortable instead.'
They summon a trolley, wheel her out
to where the nurses swirl about:
three shifts a day – all come, all go,
in a square dance, to and fro.
'We can't predict,' the doctors say.
One goes off on holiday.
Another says, 'She'll die today.'
She rallies, but he slips away.
And yet one more who can't foretell;
We saw him once – he's gone as well.
She sleeps; they wake her doing jobs;
she sleeps; they wake her up for 'obs'
(temp. and pulse); she tries once more
before she's rolled to check for sores.
The bed's a thing: it moves all day
to keep the pressure-points away;
inflates, deflates, it writhes and shakes,
like sleeping on a pile of snakes.
'She's blind and deaf,' I say; with tact
suggest they warn before they act;
I tell them all what not to do,
but they have pressure problems too.
What she has today to eat,
doesn't match the menu sheet.
She's bundled, squealing, into showers;
left propped up in chairs for hours.
'The dementia ward has a bed to spare.'
She is, I think, already there.

In a Motel

The chat of chambermaids in corridors
disturbs my rest.
I don't care who or what it was they saw.
Don't they realise I'm a paying guest?

The next-door pair's ecstatic shrieks and moans
disturb my rest.
It's not much fun for me in here alone.
Don't they think to share with other guests?

Late-night parties heard through open doors
disturb my rest.
Why must they rent their rooms to oiks and boors?
Don't they realise I'm the model guest?

Children left to squeal and play the fool
disturb my rest.
Are the leash and muzzle all that cruel?
What happened to respect for older guests?

The rush and flush of next-door's early shower
disturbs my rest.
Why cleanliness at this ungodly hour?
Must waterfalls cascade to cleanse these guests?

The memory of last night's bit of strife
disturbs my rest.
My TV up too loud? Oh, get a life!
I couldn't hear for other, thoughtless guests.

On the Lake

The sails in distant silence move
to and fro in the wind's hand;
they glide and bow, as if to weave
figures in a sarabande.

The scullers slide their smooth machine,
lever blades and draw the shell
length by length; they reach and pull,
piston-like, in parallel.

Dragon-paddlers grunt and shout;
the bully-drum their discipline;
a ragged centipede of arms;
doggedly they dig to win.

A power-boat goes hooning past,
its water-wheelies rock the swans
and carve its vandal-mark on day;
as quickly as it comes, is gone.

Now three are past, and in their wake
the drifting sails reclaim the lake.

Views of the Opera House

Dining near the Opera House
we felt inclined to tell
of metaphors and happenings
around those famous shells.

The wits were quick: 'a scrum of nuns';
'a dozen Sydney oysters'.
(That, for harbour shores, more apt
than rugby in the cloisters!)

I saw a rack of washing-up
the dishes stacked and white;
or menace in a swirl of fins,
cruising through the night.

A crouching dinosaur, perhaps,
with back of scaly plate,
turned to face its predators:
the 'Toaster' and its mate.

Utzon's shells were slim and high;
a notion of some worth;
'Can't be done!' the builders said,
and brought it down to earth.

Others finished the vision off,
which seems now to reflect
the jagged reefs of politics,
where all our dreams are wrecked.

Mowing

Mowing is a kind of meditation;
a circling of the lawn that centres soul.
On Saturdays and Sundays through the nation,
we common people seek a common goal.

Round and round, edging to the centre,
tracing through the spiral's tightening curl,
the mind on track, bound in the motor's mantra,
we turn and turn this almost Dervish whirl.

We may not be as practised as a priest,
or catch the Buddha's enigmatic smile,
but we have the pleasure, at the least,
of losing world and worry for a while.

And at the end each mower stands reborn;
the ragged soul as tidy as a lawn.

Baggage

a plane left Heathrow
two and a half hours late
but regained the time
and picked up another hour
because the luggage
was left behind

a stroke
of airline incompetence
had granted the passengers
instant enlightenment
painless non-attachment
to personal baggage
and easy travel
in higher, rarefied
realms of being

it was surprising
therefore
that when they came
down to earth
they grumbled
about their loss
clamouring for the return
of the comfortable
and familiar burdens
of their lives

Bowlers

White-robed worshippers they are:
communicants, suburban souls,
who come with gifts to celebrate
the weekend ritual of bowls.

This purity so late in life
suggests they're ready now to serve
these nobler ends. This game, though, needs
their mastery of bias, curve.

Respectfully on little mats
of prayer, like supplicants they stand;
their gifts, the shiny-pated bowls
held out before in hopeful hands.

They bow, step forward, genuflect;
send their offerings rolling out
across the green, to touch the heart,
win the end, allay the doubt.

The bowls curve in, obliquely, slow.
They knock and fall, in fortune's cast.
Impartial tapes then measure skill,
deliver judgements, first and last.

Afterwards, with bread and drink,
honour blesses worthy names;
those souls who won their day, for bowls
is the last, most reverent of games.

Reflections

I lie in a lullaby of pool,
lilted in its to and fro,
watching wave-wings idly flap
as if about to lift and go.

I lie in this embrace of cool,
lazing in its easy sway;
reflecting on the pool-side palms
hula-dancing time away.

Parrots swoop, pigeons coo;
cicadas rasp the dusk, but less
and less as light and breezes fade,
soothing the pool to quietness.

It takes so long to lie so still
that water simply mirrors trees,
the tiles show still and clear, the pool
turns to nothing – and I see.

The Jogger Justifies His Anzac Day

After a run on Anzac Day, quite late,
(at dusk, in fact), I wandered past the spot
where fresh wreaths slouched against memorial gates,
focus of the day – and I forgot.
Some placed by schools, conscripted to the cause,
others from clubs, regiments or friends;
the drift of time, the piling up of wars,
dulled old resolutions to attend.
This day, to all intents, is for the dead;
but they're no longer stirred by bands, or cheers;
they lost their lives that we might live instead,
and vindicate their gift through gainful years.
So there's some merit in my Anzac dues,
paid late, by chance, and in my running shoes.

Nashos*

It wasn't love of Menzies and his mates,
nor thought of distant president or queen;
they felt no tribal envy, fear or hate,
and held no brief for gold or gasoline.

They went because the young men always do;
they went to put their manhood to the test;
they went because their friends were going, too;
they went because their leaders thought it best.

They fought because they'd heard the Anzac drum;
they fought because their country made the call;
they bound with mates and packed down in the scrum,
picked to play the biggest game of all.

They died a distant death in wasteful war.
They died because they won a barrel draw.

* National Servicemen ('Nashos') were young men conscripted into the Australian Army for two years during the Vietnam war era. They were selected by drawing birthdays from a barrel.

The Advance*

Since we're here together in this hole,
in imminent danger of being blown apart,
the time is right to say some things I've thought
but held my tongue about this month or two.
Have I ever told you I admired
that long smooth barrel, straight and firm and true?
That well-turned butt? How much I yearned to load,
to push a round into that cosy breech,
firing to an instant's ecstasy without
the complications coming with new life?
Why not take off the safety catch, let go,
(if you take my meaning) make the most
of every moment – have a little death,
before some rocket gives us both a big one.

* It has been reported that the Pentagon carried out a six-year project researching a chemical bomb that would induce sexual attraction among enemy soldiers.

Spit Polishing

The days of buffed-up brass and blancoed belts
were gone; spit polishing remained.
We'd smear the polish on, then spit and rub,
the cloth-clad finger circling, whirling,
waltzing with a thousand tiny turns
across the leather toe;
tedious practice in pursuit of shine.
The aim – to see your face reflected there,
you a part of them, and they of you.
We sat for hours, dribbling on our boots,
taught, like Pavlov's dogs, to salivate
at the very sight of army leather.
A brush would rake the glaze, and vandalise
a week's slow work; we humbled ourselves before
the regimental life, the uniform;
the closest thing to licking boots I know.
I wasn't all that good at it, the best
had toes of glass; and when I was discharged
the army kept my would-be-glassy slippers;
no prince of arms ever called again
to fit my foot and ask my hand in war.
No fetish formed for me; I look down now
at dull-brushed shoes, with equanimity.

Sandakan Memorial*

Beneath the Chinese elms this monument
confronts us with our ageless human pain;
a jagged bronze moulds Sabah's peaks and plain,
this metal ribbon tracing the ascent
from Sandakan: two thousand men, hell-bent,
weak from thirst and fever, forced-marched to gain
the murderous intent of that campaign.
Just six would bear the pall for all who went.

What universal purpose was assured
as each man trailed his cross through jungle heat?
Was some redemption gained with each throat's cry?
Too hard to say that what these men endured,
the Calvary each trod with hopeless feet,
lifted them towards an empty sky.

* In 1945 some two thousand prisoners of war were forced-marched inland by their Japanese captors away from the coastal town of Sandakan in North Borneo (now Sabah) to avoid the advancing Allied forces. All but six died or were killed.

Stars

Someone's left the flag up;
out there in the night, in the wind;
it flaps like a dying fish, the cord
clanking against the metal pole.
Behind me, in the room, a quartet grieves
softly on the radio; and still
the flag flaps, brandishing
its faded stars. A dog barks
somewhere in the dark; a horse
snorts and thumps its foot.

The night is clear and windy.
Stars burn. The Milky Way
tracks across the night, and still
the flag flaps, its little sky
unseen, its clumsy stars
boasting our togetherness,
waving at the universe.
In the darkness I can just make out
the vines, there at the edge,
stripped of grapes, stretched,
crucified along the racks of wire.

Inside, the quartet ends; the news
comes on. There is talk of war.
The flag flaps; someone
should take it down;
take it in and fold it up;
away from the silence, the night,
and the boundlessness of stars.

On First Looking into Slater's Guide

Avocet, apostle-bird,
bulbul, booby, bristle-bird,
frigate-bird and friar-bird,
butcher-bird and lyrebird,
finches – blue-faced, crimson, star,
long-tailed, masked, the double-bar,
oystercatcher, phalarope,
oriole and pardalote,
plover, pitta, pipit, quail,
skua, roller, swift and rail,
noddy, nightjar, pilot-bird,
godwit, gull and rifle-bird,
coot and coucal, chat and chough,
crake and crane, knot and ruff,
dotterel, drongo, the barking owl,
martin, miner, mallee-fowl,
tattler, triller, swan and stork,
cassowary, kite and hawk,
shag and shoveller, tern, sitella,
stilt and stint, the little corella,
babbler, brolga, budgerigar,
kookaburra, crow, galah.

Racing Pigeons

The pigeons are out again this morning, thirty or forty of them, in a mirror-ball of flickering wings. They circle the neighbourhood again and again, the whole flock stretching and compacting, whitening as they breast the sun, darkening as they turn away. At work in the garden I have often been startled as they swung low, like a sudden wind, their shadows sweeping the lawn. They fly in silence, as intent as cyclists around a velodrome, wings whispering like tyres. There's danger, though: I've seen a pigeon miss a signal, be a moment too slow to bank or climb, and collide with another, its flight unravelling in a fluttering fall. One bird must lead, a kind of wing commander, but they all move together as if they were one thought, of one mind, one flight of imagination in the open sky.

Owl

Outside that night to finish watering,
I lit my torch, and climbing up the steps
caught sight of something on the neighbour's roof:
a shadow there, dark against the stars.

I flashed my torch – it turned its glorious eyes,
appraising this effrontery of light.
I gazed, owl-eyed – then kindly doused my torch;
and when I looked again, saw only night.

Rainbow Lorikeets

A carnival of lorikeets
is camping in our brittle gum:
a dozen or so
spruiking and squealing;
colourful as clowns,
they wear hoods
violet as night, vests
of sunset, coats
of rainforest green;
promiscuously joyful,
they chatter, clamour,
carousing all at once, or
suddenly, not at all;
they strut high branches
like wire-walkers,
do gymnastic swings
from beak and claw,
and dine extravagantly,
scattering our lawn
with nuts and twigs.
When two fly off, the others
consider this in silence,
and are gone:
to open
in some other tree.

Heron

A heron
in the still morning
places its steps

one
by one
at the lake's edge

pairing
its reflection
toe to toe

it presses ripples
from the green
willow-shade

pauses
to let stillness
gather

and stilts forward
scanning the pool
keen

to betray
its poise
its spell

with a sudden
hungry
stab

Sonnet For Sixty – 2005

What might this be? A catalogue of wins?
But modesty forbids – and hides, as well.
Much longer, though, my litany of sins.
(No gentleman, of course, would kiss and tell.)
A list of ills? So favoured of old dears?
My eyes, my bones, my veins, my skin, my glands?
The soft alarm bells ringing in my ears?
The touch of rigor mortis in my hands?
Ah no – all this is past; today's the dawn
of my new age – undoing old time's spell:
I'll shed remorse and vanity, and scorn
the lore that says I can't be old – and well.
I'm past illusion now; just watch me thrive,
and run a marathon in 'forty-five'!

Retiring

For soldiers it's pulling out of battle,
usually in disarray,
to count the dead and gauge the will
for a counterattack.

For sportsmen it's being hurt on the field
and helped or stretchered off
to polite applause, and a short announcement
later, of their condition.

For most it's giving up the desk and view
and going through the files,
seeing your working life
flash before your eyes;

it's saying goodbye to colleagues,
your other family,
knowing their silent calculations
of gain or loss;

it's shedding a moment's tears
over gifts of clocks and ties,
before the world moves on
and closes up the gap;

it's taking off your title,
handing in your keys,
and walking empty-handed
to your car;

it's becoming in a moment
an unauthorised person,
to whom the *no trespassing* signs
now apply.

Retiring is seeking our rest
at the end of the day,
to pursue our various private passions
out of the public eye.

It's being qualified by age
for a new position,
with ample prospects of promotion
to senility, and beyond.

Tanka

home
from my retirement party
a little sad
for the very first time
at taking off my tie

Seasons

He stands in the kitchen doorway, looking out
through screen-door gauze to the autumn afternoon;
it's warm and still, some roses still in flower,
the storms and heat of summer long since gone.
Retired now, he looks to life ahead;
two butterflies, from bush to bush, weave
a counterpoint in white. Trees are still;
a wren makes prinking sounds, and silvereyes
flicker in the shadow of the leaves.
Behind him, at the table, his aged mother
finger-reads her way through Sunday's news,
stories or ads – whatever takes her eye.
About to go, he hears her make a remark,
and turns, his hand pausing on the latch.

Leaves

a toddler
runs laughing
through the leaves

far too young
to comprehend
autumn

The Senior Aquarobics Class

Arriving late, I found the pool in use;
bobbing with heads, some yellow-capped, some grey;
though keen to swim, I wasn't so obtuse
I'd stand and stare, so mainly, looked away.
The young instructor danced along the side,
demonstrating movements: step and punch.
She modelled, too, what made us envy-eyed:
the lissomness of youth - ours gone to lunch.
The water smoothes and buoys; each in her place
danced her slow ballet, and each redeemed
the elegance of youth, moving with grace,
as sweet as honey, in this pool of dreams.
Until they clambered up from that rebirth,
and felt again the drag of age and earth.

98

Just two years short of her first hundred years,
my mother struggles up her Everest.
Each day, in pain, she climbs from bed, and steers
a lurching journey up the hall – in quest
of kitchen chair and medical relief.
With foggy eyes and knotted hands she sorts
her tiny tablets; spilt, they bring more grief;
her stick will fall, her glasses join the sport.
She crosses off each day – we gave her clocks
to tell her that, but she forgets they're there.
Her twisted feet need thick 'Explorer' socks.
Her shoes fall off; her arms won't reach her hair.
'People can live too long,' she said one time;
grasped her stick, and pushed on up the climb.

Two Women

Sybil
asked Zeus for eternal life
but forgot to ask for the accessory
eternal youth;
shrivelled and wizened
she was asked what she wanted
and said
I want to die

This mother
God granted a long life
unthinkable to ask for the accessory;
she suffers pain, her eyes darken,
her memories flood her understanding
she was asked what she wanted
and said
I want to live

Last Years – A Tanka Sequence

last night
her dementia attack
and a storm –
this morning rose petals
scattering the lawn

moving in
at the nursing home
her wall clock stopped –
I find batteries
for this beginning

her own room
a view of the garden
attentive staff –
surrounded with care
she spits out her food

at times
my mother mistakes me
for my dad –
at ninety-eight years
still needs to be held

the nursing home
has a grandfather clock
near the door –
long chains click down
beads in slow hands

what matter
that my mother forgets
my kindness –
we have both mastered
living in the moment

in sunlight
rugged up in her chair
she sleeps –
the clouds seem not to move
but soon enough are gone

To a Friend

We talked of sculpture once, as I recall;
I liked the Pieta, you chose The Kiss.
Sharing what impressed us most of all,
we talked of sculpture once – as I recall
it was the Virgin's helpless hand let fall
that moved me most; but now, I must confess,
we talked of sculpture once, and I recall
I never asked you why you chose The Kiss.

Tanka

after your visit
I left our cups on the bench
untouched –
not wanting to wash away
the last of the afternoon

*

noticing
at the poetry section
a woman –
I take down a volume
scan some opening lines

*

liquidambar
scattering red jig-saw leaves
all over my lawn
but I've no time for puzzles
and the wind has no idea

Professional Encounter

A nurse appears with form in hand,
and looks around – I hope, for me;
her Russian accent strokes my name;
'Come through, take off your shirt, lie down.'
The words to conjure fantasies!
She dims the lights, begins to touch;
I lie, surrendered to her skill.
A lubricant is introduced;
she probes, caresses, nuzzles, kneads.
I am pushed and turned to find
positions suited to her whim.
She maps my inner self, my soul;
I feel transparent to her eyes,
my every blemish, secret, known.
I want it so! And at the end
of this affair, she says the words
I long to hear: 'It looks all right.'
and I, at least, am satisfied.

Ticket Not To Ride

Marking my place
in a copy of Dante
I found a platform ticket

Strathfield
December 29th
1999

a ticket allowing the bearer
to say hello or goodbye
but not to travel

this one I bought
when you travelled north alone
keen to see friends

and one year later
I held another ticket
as your train pulled out

on your final journey
leaving me alone
on the empty platform

you were the adventurous one
always eager
to make the journeys

I was content
to carry bags
fetch coffee and sandwiches

I guess, one day
I'll be hustled into a carriage
bound for the underground

to take my place
wherever's been reserved
for such as me

an eternal season ticket, perhaps
on Dante's
City Circle

Moon

For thousands of years
you gave us the come-on:
'Want a good time, boys?'
you'd say, doing each month
a kind of strip tease,
unveiling your mascara-smudged
and slightly boozy face.

Finally,
we took you on;
cost a lot, though,
for a short time;
an adolescent fling, perhaps,
or someone took a dare.

We didn't go back.
Needed to settle down;
see if we could make it work
down here.
We see you go past each month
on your beat,
and you're still attractive, of course,
but we're trying to make
this relationship work.

Don't be angry.
Anyway,
where else could you go?
Saturn's too classy,
and Jupiter has seventeen.

After all,
we still respect you.
You're all we've got;
and, you never know,
if things get too hot down here
or it doesn't work out,
we might try again:
get together, establish a colony,
settle down.

We still love you.
Trust us.

Trophies

cluttering a narrow shelf
my monuments
to all my little victories
in sport and art

plaques and pennants
mugs and marble blocks
figurines on pedestals
and plastic laurel wreaths

once they gleamed
and I could see myself
reflected there, but time
has dulled that sheen

now they crowd
like an old graveyard
all angels and obelisks
with faded epitaphs

lying on the outskirts
of my life – a place
to go at times to reminisce
or clean

and wonder if they serve
a different purpose now
pointing forward
as they hand me dust

Bait

I coped with prawns, they came wrapped and dead,
and curled like hooks seemed destined for this fate;
at least they couldn't protest at the thread
of cruel barbs that turned them into bait.
The yabbies lurked in tidal flats; we'd trudge
the stinking river mud with pumps, to snort
and spurt out barrelsful, then sift the sludge
for wriggling pink – not my idea of sport.
But worst were on the point – the soldier crabs:
a rustling swarm of balls with legs; I'd look
as others scooped them up, then feign some grabs;
they threaded these alive onto the hook.
We hoped for bream and snapper on the dish,
but I remember little of the fish.

If

Someone is flying a kite; it sweeps and sways
at the end of its long line, drawing all eyes
as it tadpoles in the wind; each move displays
the struggle of earth and sky – in compromise.
The kite, though, wants the wind: to break free,
be whipped away, spire above the land
at one with urgent air, an ecstasy
untethered by familiar, caring hands.
But such adventures have another side:
the turbulence will fade to flatter air;
curious birds, or trees, will end the ride,
and dump the kite beyond the reach of care.
Better to stay, getting the balance right,
and keep as fantasy, unfettered flight.

Lines

1

on the grass in the park
four sprinklers in a row

shooting out
plumes of spray

like long-tailed birds
pheasants, or lyre-birds

turning slowly
in a measured dance

2

on the grass in the park
four sprinklers in a row

shooting out
plumes of spray

like four quills, writing
on green parchment

lines in praise
of long-tailed birds

Riddle

A floating cloud;
a muddy lake;
a hint of storm
that doesn't break.

A cowled hood
suggests my name;
friars and monkeys
much the same.

My bitter kiss
is your delight;
my lovers find
no rest at night.

And if you can't
untangle this,
take counsel from
the dragon's hiss.

(cappuccino)

Deceased Estate

The old couple's house,
just along our quiet lane,
has been sold and done over:
a vast, new house,
of white stuccoed brick,
squats on the old.
A high wall along the front
fortifies the family within;
the side garden
has been dug up,
and turf and chips laid down.
A black BMW
is sometimes out the front,
with the spare Audi
and a pristine four-wheel drive.
Outdoor tables appear
but no one seems to sit;
and two big black dogs rove
behind the cyclone wire.
Next, the drive is tiled,
iron gates arrive, polished doors,
a brass bell and numbers;
and now, today,
the finishing touch –
the first junk mail.

The Kingdom of Heaven

Close all the churches! Silence the hymns!
Discard all the Bibles! Indulge all your whims!
Saint Mark missed the mark, and forget about Paul;
the Kingdom of Heaven is down in the mall!

Chocolates, watches, wardrobes entire;
all of the goodies to which we aspire;
the mirrors, the chrome, the lights say it all –
the Kingdom of Heaven is down in the mall!

Whereas in the past we felt bad about splurges,
the impulse to spend's now the noblest of urges.
Make fashion your scripture; heed the ads' call!
The Kingdom of Heaven is down in the mall!

Everyone's young, and everyone smiles,
and everything's new, in a wide range of styles;
and the models are angels, all handsome and tall,
in the Kingdom of Heaven, down in the mall.

Who needs a god? There's a special on jeans!
And why should you wait? You'll be old at eighteen!
You can have it all now; you'll be having a ball;
in the Kingdom of Heaven, down in the mall.

So trade in your soul for that small piece of plastic;
you'll find that their terms are truly fantastic!
There's only one sin – not spending it all,
in the Kingdom of Heaven, down in the mall.

Everyday Odysseus

Homer wouldn't celebrate
our everyday odysseys
on crowded roads.
We drive each day
controlled, patrolled,
in browbeaten herds
of cowed cars,
too scared to steal
even a little speed.
For us Charybdis
is the sluggish whirlpool
of peak-hour,
and Sirens promise
penalties
without delight.
But as I slink
past the camera's
Cyclops eye,
fearing to wake it
to an angry flash,
in my heart I am always
sharpening, charring
the stake.

Cosmology – 1

At first God lived just near us, in the sky,
watching with a stern but certain eye.

Until astronomers, inviting brawls,
moved mankind from centre stage to stalls.

We had to look much further into space,
and put on spectacles to see God's face.

To hear his distant whisper we made ears;
to know his thoughts we stretched our minds light-years.

Until we reached that point from which we sprang:
the crowded egg that hatched us with a bang.

The ancient riddle's solved – although, it's odd:
the egg came first, which makes the chicken, God.

Cosmology – 2

Thanks to all cosmology has won
we hear the echoes of God's starting-gun;
there is a rumour, though, not yet denied,
the start was false – and we're disqualified.

Aspirational

the children
drink
babycinos

(that's hot
frothed
milk)

their parents
drink
decaffeinated

cappuccinos
with lo-fat
soy

working their way
up
to babycinos

Pears

1

The pear's one fruit,
but sounds a pair;
there must be another
pear in there.

2

Prone to despair
and down at heart,
life went pear-shaped
from the start.

3

A homely fruit,
but women, beware:
many a man's been lost
to the au pear.

Simplify! Simplify!

Simplify! Simplify! Beethoven scribbled in his margins and strode to greatness. Simplify! Simplify! Thoreau spoke from his bare-boards hut on Walden Pond – Let your affairs be worked on the fingers of one hand! Yes, yes, the old digital was best, I thought, as I lugged luggage, gadgets and just-in-cases. That's my dream: to make life's journey with elegant simplicity, trim and pared. I will free myself from the ache to accumulate, resist the buy-buy-babes, the fast-fat and the fly-buy-nighters. I will eschew commercial Christmas, shun the Valentine's Day massacre of taste, myxomatose the Easter bunny. Reduce! Eliminate! Simplify! To this end I have three books on the simple life, four on plain language and five on reducing clutter. I will enter a spiritual dry-dock, scrape the barnacles of resentment and regret, and sail smoothly through life. I will speak simply, omit needless words, editing to the essence. I will swap Homer for Haiku. I will shave with Ockham's Razor, rejoicing in all that is disciplined and elegant. In time, I will attain the ultimate in simplicity: boxed, labelled and stored.

Of course, one can go too far.

www.ingramcontent.com/pod-product-compliance
Lightning Source LLC
Chambersburg PA
CBHW062152100526
44589CB00014B/1799